Original title:
When Succulents Speak

Copyright © 2025 Creative Arts Management OÜ
All rights reserved.

Author: Ethan Prescott
ISBN HARDBACK: 978-1-80581-930-1
ISBN PAPERBACK: 978-1-80581-457-3
ISBN EBOOK: 978-1-80581-930-1

Succulent Serenades

In pots they chat, quite sprightly,
They gossip of sunshine, oh so brightly.
With little leaves that dance and sway,
They crack jokes in their own leafy way.

Their laughter fills the garden air,
With witty puns that none can compare.
A prickly friend joins in the fun,
Saying, "I'm sharp, but I'm not a pun!"

Secrets Beneath the Soil

Deep down where no one sees,
They share tales of wild breezes.
With roots entwined, they whisper low,
"Did you hear the one about the hoe?"

The earth is full of their grins,
As they joke 'bout gardening sins.
Worms roll their eyes, too deep to laugh,
While beetles just feel the aftermath.

Echoes of the Cacti

In a desert chat, they poke some fun,
A jocular spire under the sun.
"Why did the cactus get a date?"
"Because he's sharp but never late!"

They tease the flowers, soft and sweet,
"Your petals flop, but we can't beat!
Our armor's fierce, our wit is grand,
In this prickly world, we take a stand!"

Petals of Silence

Though silent often, they joke in sighs,
With petal secrets and spiky replies.
"A bloom so bold," one laughs with glee,
"Just wait till the night, we'll set it free!"

In stillness, they plot a whimsical prank,
A tease for the bird who can't find the tank.
"Let's leave them guessing, the flowers too bright,
We'll pop out at dusk, what a funny sight!"

The Breath of Succulents

In pots they sit with smug delight,
Whispering tales beneath moonlight.
Filling the air with a dry chuckle,
Each leaf a meme, their laughter a puzzle.

They gossip in hues of green and gray,
Beneath the sun they dance and sway.
"Water? No thanks! We thrive on drought,"
Their sassy remarks leave us in doubt.

Unspoken Wisdom of the Garden

Their spines stick out like tiny fists,
Sharing wisdom with little twists.
"Don't take life too seriously," they grin,
With roots that wiggle just beneath the skin.

In silence they boast, the ultimate trend,
Holding secrets that never bend.
"Who needs a rain dance? Let's bask instead!"
The laughter of cacti, like jokes unsaid.

Succulent Secrets

They huddle close in the sandy bed,
With a glimmering smirk, they nod their head.
"Don't mind the sun, we thrive in heat,"
A prickly bunch with humor so sweet.

"Dry humor's our game, we twist and tease,
No need for tears, we've got the breeze."
With every petal, they share a quip,
A garden full of laughter, on a sunny trip.

The Heartbeat of the Arid

In a barren patch, their colors pop,
With beats of a heart that never stop.
They giggle and snicker when you're not aware,
"Who needs a drink? Just bask and stare!"

Amongst the rocks, they hold a show,
"Drought's our jam, just so you know!"
With every glance, they wink and cheer,
In this dry kingdom, they've got no fear.

Grit and Grace in Greenery

In pots they sit, so prim and neat,
With arms all stiff, they can't be beat.
A little sun, a splash of rain,
They strut around without a stain.

With spiky hair and colors bold,
They whisper tales that never get old.
The flower crowns, they toss with glee,
"Look at us! We've got the spree!"

The Art of Stillness in Growth

In silent stands, their stories rise,
With pouting leaves and tiny sighs.
They laugh in hues of emerald bright,
While plotting dreams by moonlit light.

A little wheel of cactus thinks,
"I'm the prince of all the drinks!"
With sips of sun, they swell with pride,
Pretending they have not a guide.

Nature's Unvoiced Narrative

A succulent saga forms each day,
In quirky shapes, they dance and sway.
From tiny roots to tips that glow,
They giggle softly, 'Look at us grow!'

With spines that glisten, they're not shy,
In verdant tones, they give a sly.
"We're the drama of the yard,
And trust us, it's not even hard!"

Harmony in Parched Landscapes

In sandy beds, they find their glee,
Camel-like, they sip with spree.
They bask in sun, a saucy crew,
While ants parade with tasks to do.

With clever smiles, they share their jokes,
Among the rocks and twirly pokes.
"Life is dry but we don't mind,
A bit absurd, but still we grind!"

Whispers of the Parched

In pastel pots, they gather round,
Sharing secrets without a sound.
One boasts of roots so deep and sly,
While another brags of reaching the sky.

They sip on sun and quench with rain,
Yet still, they laugh through every strain.
Chasing dust bunnies, a hilarious sight,
In their little world, all feels just right.

Conversations Under Glass

Behind the glass, it's quite the show,
Cacti poke fun at a droopy flower's woe.
'Have you heard? Succulents get the best light!'
'Not when you're stuck in a shelf out of sight!'

Sassy leaves discuss the means to thrive,
While agaves strive to stay alive.
'You're too full of thorns,' the jade one quips,
'At least I don't need regular trips!'

Tales in Terracotta

In vessels of clay, tales come alive,
As potting mixes sing and jive.
'Stop stealing my sunshine!' a fern will yell,
'You're all just jealous of my leafy spell.'

Stretched in the sun, the aloes conspire,
Plotting mischief, their voices rise higher.
'Who needs a gardener? We're just fine!'
With cheeky grins, they sip on wine.

The Language of Leaves

Little leaves with whispers bright,
Share their gossip well into the night.
The succulents sing in a playful tone,
Mocking fallen petals left alone.

'Hear that noise?' says one with flair,
'It's just my neighbor's lopsided hair!'
They roll their eyes, oh so carefree,
Nature's jesters, wild and free.

Poetry of the Silent Succulents

In pots they sit, so cool and sly,
With whispers soft, they catch the eye.
A drink too much? They make a face,
Their plumpness shakes, a wild embrace.

The sun they soak, a lazy bunch,
In awkward poses, they'd eat lunch.
With wrinkled brows, they ponder life,
And giggle softly, sans any strife.

Thorns Tell Tales

Sharp little soldiers, standing tall,
They gossip loudly, bounce and sprawl.
With spiky humor, they crack wise,
In floral jokes, the truth is sized.

A prickly pun, a thorny tale,
Laughter blooms where cacti prevail.
They poke and prod with witty flair,
In desert lands, beyond compare.

Botanical Musings

In leafy greens, their secrets dwell,
With silent chuckles, they cast a spell.
A succulent sigh escapes the pot,
Musing on sun, and water—a lot!

They swap old jokes in shade so sweet,
While ants march by on tiny feet.
Life's a garden, and they are jesters,
Making mirth in their green festers.

The Rhythm of Resilient Roots

Roots tap dance in the soil deep,
With giggly motions, they never sleep.
Bouncing along, they wiggle free,
A funny ballet, for all to see.

They whisper secrets under the ground,
With each small ripple, laughter's found.
In every sprout, a joke takes flight,
Growing joy in the soft moonlight.

Nature's Quiet Monologue

In pots they sit, wise and green,
Whispering secrets rarely seen.
They giggle at clouds, wish for rain,
But know that sun brings no real pain.

With prickly arms, they wave good day,
As squirrels wander and children play.
Their silence is loud, a quirky jest,
To all who pass, they're nature's best.

Flourish in Silence

A cactus peeks, a little shy,
With a cheeky grin, oh my, oh my!
In the garden, they throw a bash,
With sunlight, laughter, and a splash!

They throw shade, in a cozy way,
While dancing roots play hide and sway.
With colors bright, they form a crew,
Content and spry, they know just what to do.

Drought's Serenade

In drought's embrace, they put on shows,
With twists and turns, their humor grows.
A wink from a jade plant steals the scene,
   While aloe sings of where it's been.

They shrug off woes with a leafy grin,
   As sunlight warms their spiky skin.
Who needs water when you've got style?
These garden jesters make life worthwhile.

Breaths of the Blossomed

In shadows cast, the fun begins,
Succulents wink at all life's spins.
Their roots entwined, they make a pact,
To laugh at storms, that's a fact!

Each little leaf, a story told,
In hues of green and hints of gold.
With playful glances, they charm the sun,
In whispers soft, they've just begun!

Rooted in Conversation

In the pot with my pals, we chat,
Telling tales of sun and where we're at.
"You won't believe the bug I caught,"
"Just wait till you see my greenish spot!"

We gossip and giggle, stems all a'wiggle,
Sharing stories in the light, oh so giggle.
"Did you hear about the cactus next door?"
"He keeps bragging 'bout his spikes—such a bore!"

With roots intertwined, we're all intertwined,
"Do I look thirsty?" a friend of mine whined.
Laughter echoes, we joke and we jest,
In the world of plants, we're simply the best!

Thorns and Tenderness

I've got thorns, yes that's true,
But my heart's tender—just like dew.
A prickly exterior, yet soft inside,
It's hard to find someone who'd abide!

My buddy the aloe winks with glee,
Says, "You just gotta let them see!"
"Underneath these spikes, I'm quite sweet,"
Did I mention my dessert's a treat?"

Though we poke and prod in our little patch,
Each gentle joke is quite the catch.
In our quirky garden, we thrive together,
A peculiar band through all kinds of weather.

Flourishing in Mundanity

In the daily grind, we stand so proud,
Little warriors, not too loud.
Each morning sun brings us more light,
In our humble world, we feel just right.

"Oh did you see the snail's slow race?"
"Bet you he'll win—such an ace!"
We cheer for mundane, simple things,
A laugh erupts, and joy it brings.

Beneath our soil, we wiggle and dance,
Making the most of every chance.
Even dirt can be a stage for fun,
In our succulent lives, we bask in the sun.

Secrets of the Succulent Society

In shadows deep, we whisper away,
Secrets of growth and games we play.
"Did you know that sunlight's a must?"
"And watering's key—you can't just trust!"

Through layered leaves, we share our plight,
"Got a new pot? Let's get it just right!"
Taking bets on who'll bloom first this year,
Amidst laughs and giggles, we spread good cheer.

Companions of green, we're quite the crew,
Spreading knowledge, just like morning dew.
In this society, we thrive and bloom,
With smiles and chuckles, we banish the gloom.

Murmurs of the Arid Realm

In pots so small, they sit and grin,
With spiky hair, they tease the wind.
"Water us too much, we'll hold our breath!"
Their leafy chatter, a dance of death.

"We're not needy, just a bit dry!"
Sassy little greens, reaching for the sky.
"Don't overthink, we thrive with ease!"
In sunlight's charm, they shake their leaves.

Tales of Tenacity

In desert lands where few do roam,
They plot and plan to make a home.
"Forget the rain, we're tough as nail!"
With sun-kissed skin, they tell a tale.

"Cacti with style, their spikes on display!"
Laugh at the rain; it's not their way.
"Survival's a joke, we're here to stay!"
In stubborn grace, they laugh and sway.

A Hymn to the Hardy

Brave little warriors of the dry land,
With armor thick, they take a stand.
"Bathe us in sun, that's our delight!"
Hilarious guardians, ready to fight.

"Need a hug? We prefer some light!"
Quips from the pot as day turns night.
"Don't drown us now, or we may pout!"
In shadows cast, they sing and shout.

The Unveiling of Nature's Lore

In silence woven, secrets unfold,
They gossip gently, stories retold.
"We savor the sun, like it's a feast!"
Banquet of growth, the spiny beast.

"Whispering tales of days gone by,"
"Back when we danced under the sky!"
"We're the jesters of the garden plot,"
As laughter blooms in each little pot.

Reflections in Watered Earth

In pots they sit and chat so bright,
Their gossip blooms from day to night.
With leaves like tongues they share their dreams,
Of sunny days and drizzled beams.

They argue over who's the best,
A cactus claims he's got the zest.
While jade insists with a smug little grin,
'Can we just stop? Let's not begin!'

Garden of Untold Stories

In this patch of greens, the weeds retreat,
Each tale spins softly, oh, what a treat.
The agave winks with a spine so sly,
While succulents laugh as the days pass by.

They hold secrets of the sun and rain,
Whispering softly through joy and pain.
'We've seen the world in just one pot,'
Said the thimble cactus, 'Believe it or not!'

Subtle Serenades of Succulents

Underneath the moonlit glow,
They sing of water, leaves aglow.
'More light!' yells fern, 'I need a ray,'
While others dream of a brighter day.

But wait! What's this? A squirrel's on queue,
Flirting around, stealing their dew.
All in good fun, they chuckle and squeal,
'Just bring back the sun, that's the real deal!'

The Dance of Green Shadows

In the twilight, shadows sway,
Swaying leaves steal the show today.
The aloe does a little twist,
Screaming, 'Don't forget to water this!'

A dance off starts, the pot's alive,
Those plump little greens take a dive.
With roots to the beat, they shimmy and sway,
'We're in it to win it!' they gleefully say.

Gentle Breath of Resilience

In the sun, they wiggle, sway,
With tiny grins, sharing their play.
Water's a dream, they don't need much,
Just a sprinkle, and they blush as such.

Holding secrets in their leaves,
They tell tales of summer eves.
A cactus joke, sharp but sweet,
Whispered truths where laughter meets.

Thicket of Thoughts

In a pot, thoughts intertwine,
Graphing giggles, each line divine.
"Look at me," one cactus shouts,
"I'm prickly, yet I've got clout!"

Succulents plot in verdant chat,
Pondering where the sunlight's at.
"Do we need a map or GPS?"
"Just chill out, we're the best, no stress!"

Still Voices Amongst Stones

Amongst the rocks, they softly muse,
"I've got green; you've got the blues."
A pebble nudges, "You look quite fine,
Let's paint a portrait—sip some brine!"

Meanwhile, an agave takes a nap,
Dreaming of new friends for the sap.
"Hey, who filters the light in here?"
"Not me, but I've got good cheer!"

Revelations of the Sandy Soil

In sandy homes, they plot and scheme,
Planning their next bright, sunny dream.
"Let's throw a party, let's dance and sway!"
"Bring the sun, we'll be okay!"

With laughter sprouting from each root,
They tease each other, looking cute.
"Stay hydrated, dear friend, don't be a bore!"
In whispered jokes, they root for more.

Reflections of Resilience

In pots they gossip, roots entwined,
With every drip, their wit's refined.
They lean and stretch, a quirky show,
Who knew they'd be the stars we know?

With sunshine kisses and water sips,
They twist and turn, doing little flips.
A cactus aims for that windowsill,
While the aloe's chill makes us all thrill.

Hiding tiny buds of bright delight,
They slay the gloom, bring laughter's light.
In silence wise, they dance and play,
A garden's joy in sprightly display.

So here's to greens with cheeky flair,
Living legends, without a care.
With every leaf, a tale they tell,
In whispers soft, we know them well.

A Symphony of Succulent Silence

Oh, the choir in our little nook,
Succulents sing, if you dare look!
Their silence hums a joyful tune,
Each leaf a note beneath the moon.

The jade plant chuckles as it grows,
While the rubber tree giggles, who knows?
Pot laughs echo throughout the day,
As sunlight paints their leafy ballet.

In this orchestra of bright delight,
Each little green, a starry sight.
They sway and bend, a leafy glee,
Playing the tune of harmony.

So lift your pots and join the refrain,
With every drop of joyful rain.
A symphony of quirky plant cheer,
Bringing smiles, year after year.

Heartbeats of the Hardy

A resilient crew in a sunny bay,
With hearty laughs, they frolic and play.
Prickly pals with spiky delight,
Their chatter fills the chilly night.

Each mini marvel, bold and bright,
Bounce back strong, time after night.
They boast of blooms, a colorful show,
While secretly plotting their next big grow.

With every heartbeat, a tale unfolds,
Of summer rays and winter cold.
In drought they sparkle, surviving the game,
With laughter loud, they play for fame.

So let's raise pots for the hardy crew,
Who thrive and jive with skies so blue.
In their playful world, they rule the day,
With hearts so strong, they dance and sway.

The Syllables of Succulent Shape

Round and plump, they twist and sway,
In leafy forms, they love to play.
Their curvy lines tell stories bright,
In every nook, pure delight.

Poking fun with spiky crowns,
They turn our frowns upside down.
With every curve, a giggle bends,
These little greens are faithful friends.

From rosettes to wagging tails,
Their shapes enchant with lively tales.
A mosaic of textures, bold and cute,
In equal measure, fun and astute.

So take a moment to appreciate,
The playful forms that plants create.
In every shape, a laugh awaits,
In the company of greens, joy abates.

Dialogues of Drought

A cactus chuckles at the sun,
"I'm not thirsty, just having fun!"
While the jade plant rolls its eyes,
"To sip some rain would be a prize!"

Laughter echoes in the pot,
"Why eat water? I've forgot!"
A succulent winks, a sly tease,
"Drought or not, I'll still appease!"

The aloe shouts, "I'm cooling down!"
A little sage joins, makes a frown.
"I'm dry and witty, can't you see?"
"I thrive on chaos, let it be!"

They giggle as they soak the rays,
In the sunlight's warm embrace, they play.
With every joke, a leaf does sway,
Nature's humor, come what may!

Voice of the Vivid Vines

The tendrils twist, they dance and sway,
"Who needs a drink? Let's laugh today!"
With bright green grins, they share a jest,
"Hanging around is simply the best!"

A vine declares, "I'm quite the tease,
Come play with me, and here's the keys!"
The others giggle, adding flair,
"In this garden, we're the pair!"

"Watch me climb the tallest shelf!"
Said the cheeky one, full of self.
"Catch me if you can, oh please!"
They frolic like a summer breeze.

Voices blend, like colors bright,
In their playful, leafy flight.
With vines of humor, joy unfurls,
In a world of twirls and curls!

Whispers of Green

In the stillness, a whisper flies,
"Are you thirsty?" the succulent sighs.
"I drink in sunshine, can't you tell?"
While cactus chuckles, does it well.

"Hello, my friend! You look so bold,"
"Hydration's nice, but I'm just gold!"
The gravel laughs at the plants' old bickering,
Each one feels pride in what they're delivering.

"Can we agree on playful glee?"
"Sure! Just not too much humidity!"
Whispers flutter, their leaves do shake,
As laughter echoes, the roots awake.

Underneath the moon's soft gleam,
They share their dreams, and then they beam.
In every crack, in every seam,
A world of humor, like a dream!

Conversations in Clay

Inside the pot, they chat and joke,
"I'm holding it all! I'm not just smoke!"
The soil giggles, rich and deep,
"You think you're grand? Just let me sleep!"

"With me around, you'll never die,"
Claimed the stout plant, reaching high.
"But in my shade, you ought to hide,"
The others laugh, full of pride.

A little sprout chimes in with glee,
"Can we just soak, and not decree?"
"Let's create a ruckus all around,"
These funny greens in laughter drown.

In their clay homes, with joy they spin,
A ranch of laughter, let the fun begin!
Each pot a stage, a plant's grand play,
In this garden of chatter, come what may!

Life in the Drought

In the sun, we stand so proud,
Growing tall, yet never loud.
With our spines, we guard our wit,
Who knew that dry could be quite a hit?

We soak up rays, not a single drop,
Chillin' by the garden shop.
Roots so deep, our secrets keep,
Water? Nah, we like the dry sweep!

Pot parade, we look a fright,
Wobbling under the moonlight.
Cracking jokes with our green friends near,
Guess who can survive with no sneer?

Calling cacti, come take a look,
A spiky gang with a comic book.
In the drought, we're having a blast,
Bet you wish you had us in your cast!

The Soft Murmur of Succulents

In corners bright, we share our tales,
Of sun and rain and tiny gales.
Whispering secrets of the breeze,
With a chuckle, we aim to please.

We giggle as the raindrops fall,
Drop by drop, we stand tall.
With every squishy, friendly grin,
Our humor blooms, fresh from within.

Chit chat in a pot so snug,
Meeting friends, we give a shrug.
"Did you hear? The roses weep!"
"Oh, stop it now, we're in too deep!"

With our plump bodies all aglow,
We share our wisdom, soft and slow.
Nature's jesters, dressed in green,
Together we're quite the funny scene!

Chronicles of the Resilient

In a world where water's rare,
We've got style and funky flair.
Daring droughts, we stand our ground,
With resilience that's quite renowned!

Sipping sunlight, with a grin,
We thrive where others can't begin.
Each leaf a laugh, each stem a quip,
In our kingdom, we make the trip!

When the sun decides to roar,
We just bask and ask for more.
With roots so strong, we've got the knack,
For thriving in a dry, wild track.

Let's raise our pots to the odd and strange,
Life's too short, so let's rearrange.
With humor, we turn the frown,
In this realm of green and brown!

The Silent Word of Nature

In the garden where we sit,
A gentle laugh, a little wit.
The soil whispers, "Don't you fret,"
Life's a journey, a fun duet.

Petals soft, like little dreams,
Bring joyful joy, or so it seems.
From flower highs to succulent lows,
We trade our tales, see how it flows!

Sun-kissed days, we dance and sway,
With every hour, we find our play.
In silence, we share a boundless cheer,
Nature's humor, so sincere!

So here's to the quiet cliques we've formed,
Where laughter and sunshine keep us warmed.
Nature's humor in every hue,
Join our revelry, there's room for you!

Conversations in Harmony

In sunlight's glow, we chat away,
With cacti jokes that brighten the day.
Our prickly puns, sharp and sweet,
We share them all from our leafy seat.

The aloe smirks with a witty quip,
While jade plants sway, giving a hip trip.
The pot's a stage for our green drama,
As laughter bubbles up like sweet soda llama.

Oh how we jest in our soil-made homes,
Trading barbs like garden gnomes.
Who knew thorns could poke fun this way?
We're the comedians of the clay!

So raise your leaves, let's toast today,
To pots and plots where we often play.
In our little world, all worries shrink,
Here's to the laughter that makes us think!

Wisdom Among the Weeds

In the garden's heart, we hold a sage,
A dandelion giving us wisdom's page.
"Take it easy, grasshoppers!" she'd say,
"Life's too short to rush in the fray."

The thistle chimes in, with a prickly grin,
"Don't sweat the small stuff, just let it spin!"
While daisies lean in, their petals aglow,
Sharing secrets only the weeds would know.

"Why worry 'bout weeds?" the clovers all cheer,
"We're all friends here, no need for a sneer!"
And thus under sun, with shoots on the rise,
We find wisdom hidden in nature's disguise.

So next time you walk in nature's spree,
Listen close to the chatter—be wild and free.
In every leaf, there's a tale to unfold,
And laughter of flowers will never grow old.

Arid Echoes

In the desert heat, echoes abound,
Where humor breeds in the dry ground.
A sagebrush giggles, rattlesnake grins,
In their sandy chatter, everyone wins.

Cacti wax poetic with prickly feels,
Tales of the sun and the oddest meals.
"Did you hear the one about the lost seed?"
"He found his way home when he learned to heed!"

With whispers of wisdom in arid air,
They share their joys without a care.
The yuccas boast of their dance in the breeze,
"Our moves have charm that aims to please!"

So when the heat makes you melt away,
Just tune in to what these plants will say.
In the quiet, their laughter is rich,
An echo of joy that you can't quite switch.

Nature's Gentle Whispers

Underleaf chatter in the gentle breeze,
Succulent secrets shared with ease.
A fragile sprout pipes up with glee,
"My roots are tangled, but I'm still me!"

"Oh darling, don't worry!" the fern replied,
"We all have quirks we can't hide!"
The sedum snickers, her leaves did sway,
"Let's all embrace our silly play!"

From tiny pots to big leafy beds,
We share our dreams and our garden spreads.
Each whisper a chuckle, each rustle a dance,
In nature's realm, we take a chance.

So pause for a moment, just lend an ear,
To nature's humor, bright and clear.
For in her whispers, laughter does bloom,
As we find our joy under the moon.

Voices from the Desert

Cacti whisper secrets in the sun,
Their spines stand tall, but they love to have fun.
In a jolly tone, they tease the sand,
Spouting jokes that only lizards understand.

A chubby jade plant rolls its eyes,
While a loyal aloe makes its wise replies.
"Don't be prickly! Let's dance in the breeze!"
They sway together with such playful ease.

The agave laughs and shares tales of old,
Of thirsty mischief while the sun grows bold.
"Let's put on a show, a prickly play!"
And all the cacti cheer, hip-hip-hooray!

Under the moon, they plot their next prank,
Turning dull rocks into a merry prankster's tank.
With a luminous grin and shadows that creep,
The desert delights in its laughter, not sleep.

Flora's Silent Confession

In a pot so small, a succulent sighed,
"I once had dreams, but they dried and died!"
A tiny leaf giggles at its own fate,
Saying, "Life's a jest; just wait till it's late!"

The jade plant nudges its neighbor so close,
Whispering tales like a playful, silly ghost.
"I once tried to ask a bee out for tea,
But the bee just buzzed off, left me lonely!"

Rosy petals blush, telling secrets divine,
Of wanting a hug, but it's hard to align.
"Photosynthesis? Oh please, how dull!
I dream of adventures outside the full bowl!"

With every dawn, they lift their small heads,
Sharing giggles with each morning's spreads.
Life in their world is more than it seems,
In silence, they weave the funniest dreams.

Botanical Reckoning

In the garden, a battle brews at dawn,
The succulents discuss what's going on.
"Who took my water? I'm not seeing clear!"
A grumpy pot friend slurps, "No need to fear!"

"Oh please!" scoffs the sedum, "Don't play the blame!
We all have our struggles; we're feeling quite lame.
I'm tired of sitting, just growing and green,
I want to be wild and livin' the scene!"

The eavesdropping pots join, with stories anew,
Of ambitions for life but feeling so blue.
"I wanted to climb the tallest of rocks,
But here in the shade, I just sit with the clocks!"

Then a bold little sprout shouts out with glee,
"Let's form a crew and break free, can't you see?"
With laughter and plans, they stir up the ground,
A botanical ruckus where joy can be found!

The Language of Leaves

Leaves rustle and giggle in the gentle breeze,
Chatting in colors that look oh-so-easy.
"I'm more than a green shade; I'm vibrant and bold,
Catch me in the sun when I'm wearing pure gold!"

A little succulent joins, feeling chipper,
"I dream of a life with a whole lot of slipper.
Let's hop to the pond; does anyone swim?"
But the spiky ones cringe, "Oh dear, that's too grim!"

Then the ferns chorus in delicate sings,
"Let's create a party! We'll dance with the springs.
Bring out the raindrops, it's time to unwind,
Let's celebrate life and be blissfully blind!"

In laughter and chatter, their language flows free,
An ensemble of joy in their own jubilee.
With each leafy twist, they weave tales so grand,
In the world of the plants, there's always a band.

Words of the Waterwise

In pots they sit, so full of sass,
Green giants giggle as they pass.
They whisper secrets, oh so sly,
'Water me too much, and I might die!'

With spiky smiles, they play their game,
A prickly line, yet never shame.
'Hold your horses, give us light!
Too much attention? Now, that's just fright!'

The Roots' Rambles

Down below, the roots conspire,
Stretching wide, they never tire.
'Why walk above when we can dig?
We're the stars; they're just the twig!'

They chat of dirt and all its glee,
Plotting plans for a new family tree.
'Who needs a house when you can grow?
With a little rain, we'll steal the show!'

Embracing the Thorns

In a world so fluffy, we stand proud,
With a prickly charm, we draw a crowd.
'Who needs a hug when you can poke?
Our love's a joke wrapped up in cloak!'

They giggle softly 'neath the sun,
Each spiny tale, a loaded pun.
'You've got to laugh, or you'll get pierced!
Embrace the fun, don't be coerced!'

Thickets of Thought

In the garden of chatter, ideas bloom,
A tangle of thoughts in every room.
'Let's sprout our dreams like little seeds!
Just don't forget to water our needs!'

With witty ferns and sage advice,
They ponder life, that wondrous dice.
'Thoughts may twist, but they rarely tangle,
Let's dance through chaos; oh, what a jangle!'

Green Haven of Soliloquies

In a pot, they chuckle, it's quite a sight,
With little spines, they grip so tight.
A cactus says, 'I'm prickly but wise,'
While others giggle with leafy sighs.

They whisper secrets, in hues so bright,
'Two drops of water, oh what a delight!'
The aloe rolls eyes, tired of the chat,
'Just give me sunshine, and a good old mat!'

Who knew green things could talk like this?
In their leafy world, they seldom miss.
The laughter flows with each sunny day,
In a green haven where they play.

So raise a glass to the friends of green,
With tender quips that are rarely mean.
In this garden's realm of jovial cheer,
Those succulent souls are always near.

The Narrative of Nature's Veins

A jade plant winks, with a flick of a leaf,
'Just look at my roots, beyond belief!'
While the string of hearts rolls into a spin,
'Love me or leave me, I'm destined to win!'

In the bright sun, they take a stand,
Plotting their tales in this sun-kissed land.
A barrel cactus boasts, 'I'm tough for sure,'
But secretly wishes for good ol' allure.

With every whisper, the soil does gleam,
Their stories intertwine, like a wild dream.
'What's your secret?' the succulent asks,
'I simply thrive, that's all, no big tasks!'

So gather 'round, join the green brigade,
In whispers of nature, they serenade.
Unraveled tales, both funny and sweet,
In the world of green, life can't be beat.

Silent Soliloquies of Leaves

In a corner, there's a witty little sprout,
With every quip, it's hard not to shout.
'Can you hear the silence?' the echeveria grins,
It's filled with chatter, oh where to begin?

'A sprinkle of water, and look at us grow!'
The jade laughs softly, 'Just take it slow.'
'And when it rains, oh what a mess!'
The succulent smirks, 'But I love the dress!'

These leaves exchange glee, not one is demure,
A world of whispers, so lively and pure.
Each moment's a story, a tale to delight,
In this silent dance, there's so much light.

So tap your toes to the rhythm of green,
A playful dance in their leafy routine.
For in every whisper, and every cheer,
Nature's laughter is always near.

Awakening the Desert's Heart

Beneath the sun, in sandy terrain,
A prickly pear claims its spot, quite vain.
'Why so glum?' the agave will tease,
'I'm here to brighten your prickled unease!'

'Oh, the drama!' laughs a happy little tree,
'Just soak in the rays, that's the key!'
While the golden barrel starts to hum,
A riddle of laughter, here it comes!

In a world of sunshine and playful mirth,
These desert dwellers are given new birth.
Each day anew, fresh tales to tell,
In the heart of the desert, all is well!

So raise your eye to the cacti so spry,
Their quirky lives will never be shy.
With every sunbeam and breeze that blows,
The desert blooms with the joy it knows.

Desert Dreams Unfold

In the heat of the sunny day,
Cacti gossip in their own way.
"Did you see that bee?" one did cheer,
"I think he wants to join us here!"

"Why stand so tall?" a small plant asks,
"Are you showing off your leafy tasks?"
"Just trying to catch the clouds above,
And maybe score a bit of love!"

"A lizard turned the corner, oh dear!
Do we look good? Should we shed fear?"
"I'm more worried about the wind,"
Said one in a pot, with a stem so slim.

Under a moonlit, silver glow,
Succulents laugh, with secrets to sow.
The desert's alive with tales so grand,
Of prickly banter in the sand.

Conversations with the Cacti

Three prickly friends on a sunny ledge,
Argued daily, and made a pledge.
"Who told you to wear those spines?"
"I think it's cute," one plant opines.

"I prefer a soft touch; less is best,"
Said a smooth leaf without a quest.
"Foolish! We thrive on rough terrain,
Who wouldn't want to be so insane?"

A tumbleweed rolled by, all aloof,
"Your drama's a riot—get on the roof!"
Laughter exploded, oh what a sight,
As cacti conversed deep into the night.

"Next time a bird lands here, my friends,
I'll show him our moves—let's make amends!"
Off they went, with a clumsy dance,
In the desert, where nothing's by chance.

The Quiet Symphony of Succulents

Amidst the stillness of sun-soaked earth,
A tune arises, a quirky birth.
"I'm a fan of jazz," said the Aloe,
"Swing those leaves, let's start the show!"

A round of applause from the sandy crowd,
Where cacti wobbled, feeling proud.
One, two, three! With rhythm they sway,
In their own way, they dance and play.

"Can you hear that?" asked old Agave,
"A melody hints at the bold and bravy!"
"Just a breeze," sighed a moonlit friend,
"Or perhaps the neighbors, trying to blend."

Yet night after night, they'd gather and hum,
Creating a symphony, oh so numb.
With laughter and joy in each little note,
The garden would sway, like a happy boat.

Messages from the Sun

The sun peeked in, all morning bright,
"Hey, you green folks, ready for flight?"
"We're rooted here!" shouted a plucky guy,
"Not going anywhere, and that's no lie!"

"Let's stretch our arms, soak in that glow!"
Said a daring jade with a vibrant show.
"Is it too much? I feel quite bold!"
As laughter bounced off leaves of gold.

"Don't forget sunscreen!" a wise old sage,
"Or you'll end up in a prickly cage!"
The sun just chuckled, "You silly things,
You're tougher than most; you have your bling!"

So every day they'd shout with glee,
Rooted in fun, as life should be.
Each ray a message, warm and bright,
Resilience blooms in the morning light.

The Landscape of Listening

In a garden where laughter sprout,
A cactus jokes, 'What's this about?'
With prickly puns and silly chat,
They tickle the sun, like a playful hat.

The jade plant whispers, 'Don't be shy,
I've seen worse than you, just pass by!'
With wrinkled leaves and a radiant grin,
They cheer each other, let the fun begin.

In pots they gather, stories they weave,
Of wild adventures, you'd never believe!
They roll their eyes at the busy bees,
Laughing at dreams on the evening breeze.

So listen closely, don't miss the show,
These little green Jokers put on a glow.
In their world of puns and joyful rhymes,
Every leaf giggles through the sunny times.

Echoing Silence in Pots

In a still room, a succulent sighs,
'Are we plants or are we spies?'
It watches the humans rush and run,
'Let's play a game, we'll have some fun!'

A good old aloe mutters in glee,
'While they're busy, let's brew some tea!'
With tiny cups made of clay so neat,
They clink and cheer, this is quite a treat.

The air is thick with laughter and joy,
As they plot to prank the old garden boy.
With a wink and a nod, they set the scene,
'A plant's got to hustle to keep it green!'

After their antics, they all hold hands,
Roots intertwined, like a rock band.
In their secret pot, they share a toast,
To whispers and laughter, they love the most.

Flourishing Murmurs

Under the sun, they dance and spin,
With every breeze, they break into grins.
'Leafy gossip, oh what a treat,
Did you hear what juicy tales we repeat?'

A rosette chuckles, 'I heard it last week,
A lizard on a quest for a shiny cheek!'
The others roar with laughter so bright,
As stories take flight, like kites in the night.

There's drama between the pebbles, it's true,
One says the other cheated on the dew.
With witty comebacks, they fire and zing,
In the world of greens, they rule like a king!

They flourished together in soil and sun,
Each little quip, like a loaded gun.
So next time you peek at your leafy friends,
Remember their joy as the laughter never ends.

Resilience in Every Leaf

In the pot, there's a story profound,
A thorny tale of friendships found.
'We may be small, but listen close,
Our hearts are strong, we'll forever boast.'

A spiky friend greets the morning light,
'Did you hear my last joke? It's out of sight!'
With vibrant hues, they flash and gleam,
Spreading joy like a wild daydream.

A crowd of green, all giggles and cheer,
'Why do we thrive? It's perfectly clear!'
They trade their wisdom, oh so spry,
Each leaf a champion, beneath the sky.

So rise and shine with a touch of mirth,
For in every petal lies laughter's worth.
In rooms of silence, they stand so tall,
With comedy and courage, they conquer all!

Cacti's Quiet Verse

In the corner, a cactus stands tall,
Whispering secrets, no one hears at all.
With spikes for a mouth, it tells silly tales,
Of mischief and mayhem in the desert gales.

It dreams of a dance, with a prickly partner,
Who waltzes too hard, leaving only a splinter.
In the moonlight, they sway to the stars' light,
A fiesta of spines, what a hilarious sight!

Under the sun, they plot a grand play,
Using sand as their stage, come join their array!
With laughter like rain, they shower the scene,
As the audience shifts, both green and serene.

So next time you see them, don't look away,
They're bickering softly, in their prickly ballet.
Behind every spine, there's a joke to unfurl,
A world full of giggles, full of green whirl!

Echoes in Potting Soil

In pots full of whispers, where roots intertwine,
The soil sings softly, it's party time!
Little plants giggle beneath the earth's due,
Sharing their stories, as only they do.

A succulent shouts, 'I'm the chief of the lot!'
While another replies, 'You're just a fine pot!'
Each chuckle resonates, right under your feet,
As they swap their wisecracks, all bitter and sweet.

The tiny ones giggle, the big ones just grin,
As earthworms join in with a wiggly spin.
Together they hum, a symphony loud,
In the potting soil, they feel oh-so proud.

So take off your shoes, let your toes feel the dirt,
Join the little plants, shake off all that hurt.
In the garden of laughter, we find pure delight,
As echoes of giggles dance on through the night.

Drought's Gentle Dialogue

In the heat of the day, a wise old sage speaks,
To a sleepy-eyed pebble, as both take their leaks.
'Have you felt the thirst? It's quite the affair!'
The pebble just chuckles, 'I've never a care!'

'You should listen closely, there's wisdom in drought!'
The cactus interjects, 'I'll drink what I sprout!'
With humor so dry, they weave their bright tales,
Of surviving in sand, while the sunlight prevails.

They share their best tricks, how to soak up the sun,
And how to hide laughter when the days start to run.
A wind-borne gust sends a tickle to all,
As the drought chats away, with its friendly old call.

So next time you fret, 'There's no water to find!'
Remember the laughter that drought leaves behind.
For in every dry moment, a giggle's at stake,
With cacti and pebbles, let's dance for fun's sake!

Tales from the Sun-Baked Earth

On sun-baked terrain, the story unfolds,
Where laughter grows wild as the sun-gold molds.
A tumbleweed rolls, with a chuckle or two,
'The more we roll round, the more skies are blue!'

A sunbathing lizard whispers jokes in a dance,
'Why dread the heat when you can have a chance?
To bask in the glow and giggle away,
While shadows are long, let the humor play!'

Nearby a firm agave stands rooted and wise,
Sharing tall tales with the sweet summer flies.
'Life isn't just prickly; it's quirky you'll see,
When friends are around, let loose, let it be!'

So gather your sun hats and join in the cheer,
For tales from the earth, they bring everyone near.
With laughter unending, in the warm desert breeze,
Let's dance in the sunlight, and do as we please!

The Quiet Bloom

In pots they sit, so calm and stout,
Whispering secrets with every sprout.
Their spines are sharp, but so are their jokes,
They giggle softly, these green little folks.

A cactus told me to keep my cool,
While the jade plant mocked me in the pool.
"Life is better when you're well-fed,"
Chortled the aloe, poking my head.

When storms pass by, they drink it all,
With roots so firm, they never fall.
"Hey, did you know we're low-maintenance?"
A roomful of laughter, their clever stance.

So when you think it's only a plant,
Just peek in close, they're quite gallant.
In every leaf, a joke is spun,
Trust me, their humor is second to none.

Messages from the Succulent Realm

They send their notes on a sunny breeze,
"Water us nice, but please, not the seas!"
With little grins, they lean to the light,
Telling tales of how they survived the night.

The rosette chuckled, "I'm no drama queen,
My leaves are fab, but my thorns are mean."
A pebble in the pot snickered loud,
"Beauty and guts? We're quite the crowd!"

The string of pearls winked, a cheeky sight,
"Just call me when your plans go tight!"
With each new sprout, they bring us cheer,
In the language of plants, humor is clear!

So lift your cup and toast them well,
For they share their stories, you can't dispel.
When you think they're quiet, take another look,
In every green leaf, there's fun in the book.

Stories in Stillness

In the corner of the room they dwell,
Telling stories that plant folks tell.
A succulent whispers, squeaky and bright,
"Never sweat it, we sleep at night!"

They gather round, their leaves all aglow,
"Who needs a spa? We put on a show!"
With every sip of rain, they start to grin,
You can hear their humor, like a playful spin.

"Why did the garden bench go away?"
Asked the jade plant, in a snarky way.
"To get some rest without all the fuss,
Or maybe to chill with the glorious cactus!"

In stillness, they plot their subtle schemes,
Entrapping our hearts with whimsical dreams.
So when the world shouts and you feel tense,
Just sit by a succulent, it all makes sense.

The Wisdom of Plump Petals

With wisdom thick as their plump green leaves,
They teach us patience, but love to tease.
"Do you know why we sit here so neat?"
"Because we learned to slow down and not compete!"

The cheery echeveria gave me a glance,
"We don't need haste, we relish the dance."
While the succulent sage, wise and round,
Spoke of patience, stories profound.

"Pot bound? No worries, we're all in style,
Just take a moment, let's chat for a while."
Their leaves swayed lightly, a gentle sway,
With laughter in air, they brightened my day.

So here's a toast to the plump and bright,
Who dance in silence, in sheer delight.
When life gets chaotic, just look for a friend,
In every petal, good vibes they send.

Echoes of the Parched Palms

In a pot full of sun, they shout with glee,
"Water us now, we're craving a spree!"
Their roots wiggle, their leaves in a twist,
"Who needs a shower? We've got the mist!"

"I saw a cactus wear sunglasses too,"
Said the hawthorn, feeling quite the view.
"That prickly fashion is all the rage!"
Complained the succulents, stuck in their cage.

"Did you hear, they call us desert stars,"
Chortled the jade, while sipping on jars.
"Oh please! More like houseplants in a vase,"
Snickered the aloe, all smug in its place.

"At night, we throw leaf parties you see!"
Cried out the agave, grinning with glee.
"And when we hydrate, we dance in delight,"
They giggled and twirled, a joyous sight.

Petals of Persistence

Once a tiny seed, I broke through the ground,
Wiggled and jiggled, looked all around.
"Hey there! Join us! Don't be so shy,"
Chirped the eager sprout, "Come give it a try!"

With sunlight and dirt, we share a good chat,
In our little garden, we're all quite the brat.
"I can't stand the shade, it gives me the creeps,"
Said a feisty little bloom, in her colorful peeps.

"Do we bloom at night or is that just a dream?"
Wondered the sage, with a quirky gleam.
"The moon must be jealous of all our charms,"
Laughed the bright marigold, with her sunny arms.

"Let's pitch a fit if the rain doesn't pour,"
Wailed the sunflower, "we'll scream and implore!"
But in every storm, we just soak it all in,
Chuckling together, with nature we win.

Green Gossips of Growth

In the still of the night, whispers arise,
"Did you see that bug? It's really quite wise!"
Gossip travels fast through stems and leaves,
"Shhh! Don't let the gardener catch our thieves!"

"Did you hear, Prickly Pete found a new friend?"
Asked the bright fern, with a voice to lend.
"Yeah, he's been telling tales of the drought,"
Scoffed the succulent, "I doubt that's best thought!"

"Who needs a filter when you're this cute?"
Hooted the jade, all dressed in a suit.
"When your leaves shimmer like diamonds at dusk,"
"It's hard not to brag, in friendship we trust!"

From pots all around, a chorus rang loud,
"We're the quirky greens, and we're oh so proud!"
With petal-lined voices, they laughed and they swayed,
In their garden of joys, where sunshine played.

Dialogue Amidst Thorns

In a patch of prickers, a meeting took flight,
Cacti convened under the soft, starlit light.
"Let's talk about life, our favorite way,"
Whispered a rose, "and how not to sway."

"I'll tell you a secret," said one with a grin,
"We thrive on good jokes, let the fun begin!"
"But do watch your thorns, they poke and they prod,"
Chortled the lily, while spinning a nod.

"Who invited the bee? He's buzzing so loud,"
Complained the old thyme, feeling quite cowed.
"Relax, he's a friend, just dancing away,"
Bee-laughs the daisy, in her sunny ballet.

With laughter erupting, they chuckled with zest,
"I suppose even thorns can enjoy a jest,"
Amidst all the prickles and banter so bright,
Friendship was blooming — what a comical sight!

www.ingramcontent.com/pod-product-compliance
Lightning Source LLC
Chambersburg PA
CBHW070318120526
44590CB00017B/2730